T0123405

Pathways to a Closer Walk

Bible Analogies to Nourish Our Personal Relationship with God

(A guide for personal or small group use)

JAMES A. BLAINE

Copyright © 2019 James A. Blaine.

All rights reserved. No part of this book may be used or reproduced by any means, graphic, electronic, or mechanical, including photocopying, recording, taping or by any information storage retrieval system without the written permission of the author except in the case of brief quotations embodied in critical articles and reviews.

WestBow Press books may be ordered through booksellers or by contacting:

WestBow Press
A Division of Thomas Nelson & Zondervan
1663 Liberty Drive
Bloomington, IN 47403
www.westbowpress.com
1 (866) 928-1240

Because of the dynamic nature of the Internet, any web addresses or links contained in this book may have changed since publication and may no longer be valid. The views expressed in this work are solely those of the author and do not necessarily reflect the views of the publisher, and the publisher hereby disclaims any responsibility for them.

Any people depicted in stock imagery provided by Getty Images are models, and such images are being used for illustrative purposes only. Certain stock imagery © Getty Images.

Interior Image Credit: c. Fotosearch.com

Scripture quotations are taken from the King James Version.

ISBN: 978-1-9736-5626-5 (sc)
ISBN: 978-1-9736-5627-2 (e)

Library of Congress Control Number: 2018910625

Print information available on the last page.

WestBow Press rev. date: 4/22/2019

To

Wandalou
My dear wife and helpmeet

and

Rev. Charles Wheeler Sr.
Rev. Richard Laubenheimer,
partners in ministry

Contents

Relationship Analogies in Scripture

Introduction

By divine design, we are created to be in a personal relationship with God—to walk with him—and to know him personally. Jesus echoed the familiar Old Testament commandment—and God's personal call—in Deuteronomy 6:5 when he spoke in a temple discourse. "Thou shalt love the Lord thy God with all thy heart, with all thy soul, and with all thy mind. This is the first and great commandment" (Matthew 22:37–38).

It is written that Enoch, the seventh from Adam, "walked with God" (Genesis 5:24). Through the Old Testament prophets, God called the people of Israel to a relationship with himself. Micah wrote: "What doth the Lord require of thee but to do justly, and to love mercy, and to walk humbly with thy God?" (Micah 6:8). Jeremiah spoke: "Thus saith the Lord: ... let him who glorieth glory in this, that he understandeth and knoweth me" (Jeremiah 9:23–24).

In his ministry, Jesus called, "Follow me," and "Come unto me," to invite those hearing him to a personal relationship with himself. To all those who followed him and became a part of his kingdom, he gave the gift of eternal life, which he defined in John 17:3: "And this is life eternal, that they might know thee, the only true God, and Jesus Christ, whom thou hast sent." Thus, the Christian life is not primarily based upon a knowledge *about* God, but is, essentially, upon *knowing* God personally. Or, as commonly put in other settings: "It's not what you know; it's who you know."

Imbedded throughout the Bible are several **analogies** that portray the relationship between Jesus Christ and the believer. These analogies are drawn from familiar living and simply teach their truth by using the age-old method of proceeding from the known to the unknown.

This lesson series is composed to enable each believer in Christ to "grow in the grace and knowledge of our Lord and Savior Jesus Christ" (2 Peter 5:18), and is intended to guide the user down a pathway toward a closer walk in his or her relationship with Christ. Each study concludes with a time to reflect upon its meaning, with a hymn or song to ponder, and with an invitation to compose a personal prayer based upon that analogy.

The Basics of a Personal Relationship

1. A relationship begins when two persons meet and become involved with each other.

2. A healthy relationship is an association with another person within an atmosphere of familiarity, warmth, trust, and cooperation.

3. Common ground between two persons in a relationship develops over time. A certain structure and limits to the relationship come to be agreeably understood.

4. Every relationship needs to be cultivated, nurtured, and sustained by communicating with each other, by reordering one's priorities, and by investing one's time, money, concern, or energy in each other.

5. A relationship does not remain static; it is dynamic and is characterized by either growth or decline.

6. A healthy relationship is only possible within compatible goals and lifestyles.

7. In a healthy relationship, persons will not use or exploit one another but will seek to enhance the wellbeing and worth of each other.

8. One cannot relate to another person by proxy; personal contact is necessary.

9. Self-understanding and personal development occur in a relationship with another person, who, then, serves as a mirror, so that one may observe his or her own self.

Understanding the Relationship Analogies in Scripture

- Relating partners in scriptural analogies are like the senior and junior partners in a business. They each make their own distinctive contribution to the relationship, and they complement each other.

- The "senior" partner (God the Father, or Jesus Christ) in each analogy provides responsible leadership and indicates the proper place or activity of the "junior" partner.

- The "junior" partner (the believer) in each analogy is responsible for being respectful, dependent, submissive, and obedient.

- The relationship in each analogy is marked by some appropriate interaction between the two partners and leads ultimately to some positive resolution.

- The partnering relationship is always beneficial to both partners and always shows how God values or loves the "junior" partner.

- Sometimes friction, pain, or other unpleasantness for the "junior" partner is unavoidable in the development of the relationship.

- The relationship in the analogy can deepen (by cultivation) or may deteriorate (by abuse or neglect).

The Yoked Life

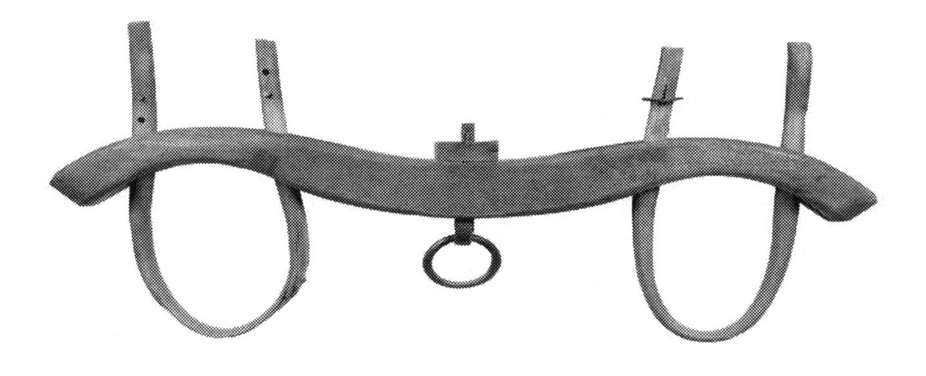

The society of Christ's day was largely agricultural, and the yoking of animals for plowing or pulling was a common practice. Although Christ was teaching a spiritual lesson, his reference to a yoke was something to which his listeners could relate. While in biblical times a yoke was used to hitch together either oxen or donkeys (compare Deuteronomy 22:10, Amos 6:12), in modern times we normally associate a yoke with a pair of oxen. Yoked oxen can currently be found in demonstrations at certain historical farm preserves (e.g., Billings Farm, Woodstock, Vermont; or Farmer's Museum, Cooperstown, New York). Perhaps someone can describe having actually seen a yoke being used.

1. Read Matthew 11:28–30, perhaps from more than one Bible version.

   Christ uses what three verbs of invitation to those hearing him?

   1.________________ 2.________________ 3.________________

What obvious response is expected to his three-part invitation?

____

____

____

In the Bible's original language, these three verbs are in the imperative mood, which signifies what?

____

____

____

2. To whom is this invitation given? (See Matthew 11:7 and 11:28.)

____

Why was it offered to them? ____________________

____

____

3. What does Christ twice promise to those who accept his invitation?

____

Compare the promise of "rest" in Ruth 1:9 and 3:1, and in Hebrews 4:1–11. What is meant by "rest"?

____

____

4. In verse 29, Christ refers to "my yoke." To what other yoke might this be contrasted? (See Matthew 23:2–4.) Note also the yoking of people in Philippians 4:3.

5. If it is assumed that a yoke has two openings, then who are to be the two occupants of Christ's yoke?

6. While an animal's yoke may be tight-fitting and applying pressure, note the paradox in Christ's statement about "my yoke."

7. What does Christ reveal about himself in verse 29? Why does he speak of himself this way?

Reflection

How and when does a person become yoked with Christ? ___________

How does a decision to be willing to become yoked with Christ differ from one to become a church member?

____

____

____

____

____

____

____

Note that Christ's invitation to "come" does not include any specific "do's or don'ts." But what is implied is simply—that a relationship with Christ will produce definite changes in the life of a person yoked with Christ.

What are the implications of a Christ-yoked life?

____

____

____

Can you add any more implications to the following suggestions?

- There is a nearness to Christ with "nothing between."
- One senses an inner assurance of forgiveness and of being at peace with God.

- One learns to be obedient to Christ's directions.
- Any obstacle, threat, or burden experienced is faced jointly with Christ.
- One may be lonely in some life circumstance but never alone.
- There will be an ever-deepening acquaintance with the Lord.
- Anything that would displease Christ must be avoided.
- Restrictive limits actually protect us.
- Being yoked with Christ enables us to accomplish meaningful tasks.
- Nearness to Christ allows special communication privileges with him.
- Certain responsibilities are entrusted to the yoked believer.

____

____

____

____

____

Christ's invitation to "come," "take his yoke," and "learn" is really an invitation to establish and experience a personal relationship. Any person may now exchange the heavy bondage of sin for a binding yoke with Christ—the Savior. One's obedient response to this invitation signifies the beginning of a personal relationship with Christ.

To promote a clearer understanding of this yoked, redeemed relationship with Christ, the Bible uses several analogies drawn from everyday life. Each analogy is as understandable today as it was in biblical times.

As we study each analogy in this study series, they will provide special insights into the nature and dynamics of one's relationship with Christ and will illustrate some facet of the personal interaction between Christ and a redeemed believer.

The Creator and the Creature

If you invented, designed, financed, and manufactured a special new machine, would you not expect the following as a result of your work and investment:

- that the machine would operate efficiently?
- that it would accomplish the task for which it was designed?
- that it would be a profitable investment?

- that it would always belong to you?
- that you would reserve the right to change it, use it, or set it aside?

What similarity might there be, then, to the Creator's design and creation of a human being?

Ponder the expectations that our Creator has concerning his new human creature and the implications of a relationship with him.

1. Examine the account of human creation in Genesis 1:26–27, 2:7, and 5:1–2.

   In Genesis 1:26–27, what phrase is repeated three times?

   ____

   ____

   What significance do you see in this repetition?

   ____

   ____

   What suggestion is there in these scriptures of the intended relationship between the creature and the Creator?

   In Genesis 2:7, what two elements did God use to create a human?

What significance is there to us in the use of those two elements?

In Genesis 1:28–29, 2:15–17, and 3:8–9, what functions or tasks did the Creator intend for his new creature to perform?

2. How do the following scriptures confirm or augment the account of human creation?

   Job 10:8–12 ______________________________

   Psalm 139:13–16 ______________________________

   Job 33:4–6 ______________________________

   Jeremiah 1:5 ______________________________

   Psalm 119:73 ______________________________

3. How is the Creator's work affirmed in the following scriptures?

   Ecclesiastes 12:1 ______________________________

   Isaiah 40:28 ______________________________

   1 Peter 4:19 ______________________________

4. Read Mark 12:28–30. When Jesus was asked to name the greatest commandment in the law, what was his answer?

5. Note the similarities to his answer in:

   Deuteronomy 6:5, 10:12, and 30:6 ______________________________

   Matthew 22:37 ____

   Luke 10:27 ____

6. What does this greatest commandment say about a relationship with our Creator?

7. How do "heart, soul, mind, and strength" differ from each other?

8. What are the implications of this commandment for me?

   ____

   ____

9. How should the human creature respect the other parts of the Creator's creation and be a responsible steward of all of God's handiwork?

   - Animals—for food, transportation, clothing, tools, amusement, companionship, etc.

     ____

     ____

- All plant life—for food, clothing, comfort, beauty, healing, etc.

___

___

- All minerals and elements—for air, water, shelter, soil, and materials for living.

___

___

- Heavenly bodies in space—to further generate awe for all creation.

___

___

Reflection

Read Psalm 8 as a worshipful prayer to the Creator for the glories of his creation.

___

___

___

Read, sing, or listen to one of the following songs:

- "He's Everything to Me"
- "How Great Thou Art"
- "Down from His Glory"
- "The Wonder of It All"

- “Morning Has Broken”
- “Immortal, Invisible, God Only Wise”
- “The Great Creator”
- “This Is the Father’s World”
- or, ______________________________

Compose your own prayer, as a creature praying to the Creator.

____

____

____

____

____

____

____

____

____

____

A sample prayer:

> O glorious Creator, as a creature fashioned by your hands, I am in awe of who you are and of all that you have made. You have made me aware that it was you who brought me into existence and gave me life, and who sustains my life from day to day and even from minute to minute. As I ponder what you have invested in me, something deep within my being wants to return my gratitude to you. Thank you for making me, and for

allowing me to live on your earth. May my life prove to be a good return on your investment in me through the saving grace of the Lord Jesus Christ. In his name, Amen.

The Shepherd and the Sheep

All through the centuries, and even in our "high-tech" age, sheep have always needed a shepherd to care for them. In this interesting relationship between man and animal, a special bond develops between them. Beginning in Genesis with Abel, references to sheep and their shepherds are found in half of the books of the Bible. Of all the relationship analogies, this one is used most frequently—whether referring to the people of Israel or, later, to the followers of Christ.

1. From your knowledge of sheepherding, what are the functions of the shepherd, and what qualities make for excellence in that task?

____

____

____

2. From your knowledge of sheep, in what ways are sheep similar to people?

____

____

____

3. Read Psalm 23. What does the shepherd/sheep analogy teach about our relationship with God?

____

____

4. Why has this psalm become one of the more familiar and beloved portions of the Bible?

____

____

____

____

____

____

5. Read John 10:1–18, 27–28. What are the actions of the shepherd, and how do the sheep respond?

____

____

____

____

____

____

6. Identify to whom the persons in the John 10 passage may be referring to?

   - shepherd = ______________________________
   - hireling = ______________________________
   - sheep = ______________________________
   - stranger (thief) = ______________________________
   - gatekeeper = ______________________________
   - sheep not of this fold = ______________________________

7. Read Luke 15:1–7. What additional teaching about the shepherd/ sheep relationship is found in this parable?

____

____

____

____

____

8. In Christ's statement "I am the good shepherd," is there some connection with Ezekiel's message to Israel in chapter 34? (Especially note verses 11–15.)

____

____

____

____

____

____

9. Read and examine some of the other scriptures that contain the shepherd/sheep analogy and call attention to any new insight:

Psalm 100, John 21:15–17 ______________________

____

Isaiah 53:6–7 (Compare with Acts 8:32), Hebrews 13:20 ________

____

Matthew 9:36, 1 Peter 2:25 ____________________

____

Matthew 10:16, 1 Peter 5:2–4____________________

____

Matthew 25:31–33 _____________________________

____

Reflection

What can you learn from this shepherd/sheep analogy that will help you grow in your own relationship with Christ?

____

____

____

____

____

Read, sing, or listen to one of the following songs:

- "Gentle Shepherd"
- "The Lord's My Shepherd"
- "Shepherd of Love"
- "The Ninety and Nine"
- "Only Believe"
- "My Shepherd Will Supply My Need"
- or ________________
- "The New 23rd"
- "Savior, Like a Shepherd"
- "I Was a Wandering Sheep"
- "His Sheep Am I"
- "One Flock, One Shepherd"
- "Like a Lamb Who Needs a Shepherd"

As a sheep in the Lord's flock, what could be your prayer of thanksgiving and petition to the Good Shepherd?

The Head and the Body Member

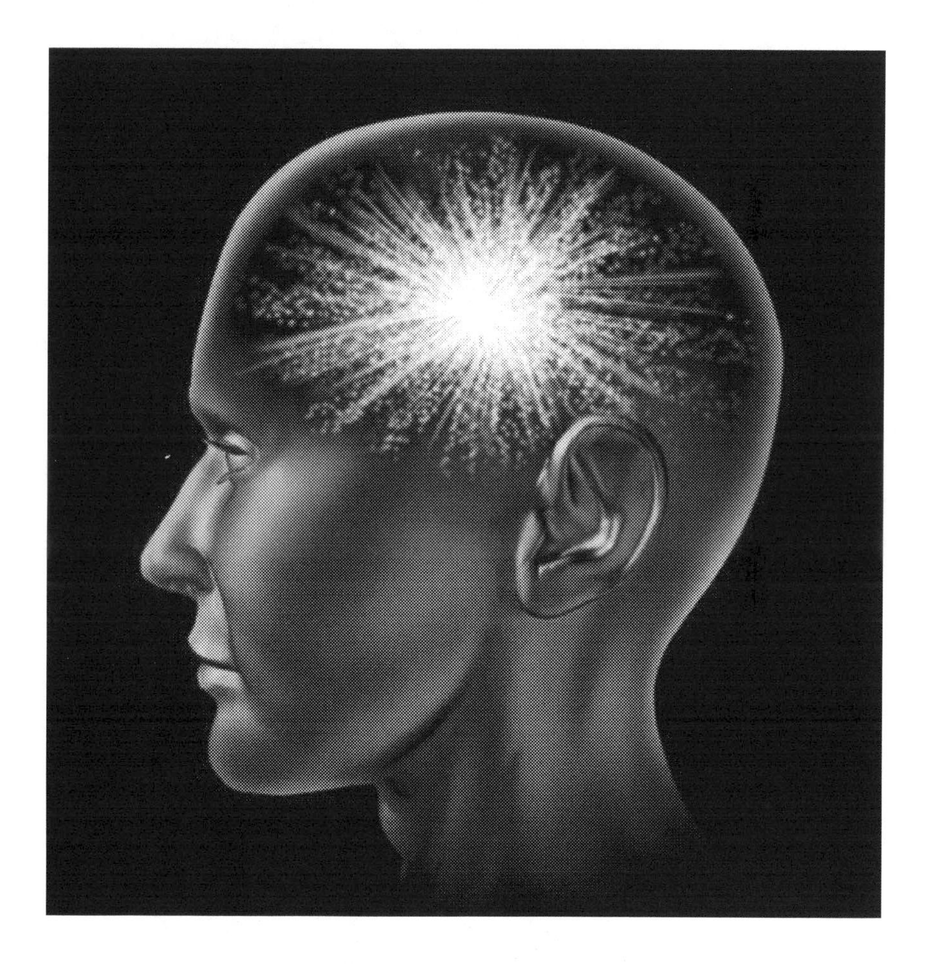

Living every day with our physical bodies, we use their many parts and systems without really thinking about how they work. In this earthly part of us, all of our functioning systems are coordinated in a sophisticated symphony, enabling us to perform various tasks. Truly the human body is a wonderwork of design and is intricate beyond our full understanding.

Initiating actions and controlling movement is all done by the head. The brain sends impulses along nerve pathways, and our body parts respond to accomplish a designated task.

1. When a person reaches out to grasp an object, what body parts or systems must function in order to accomplish that action? How do the head and body members interact in that function? Trace the sequence of the functioning of the involved body parts (e.g., the optic nerve must first relay information to the brain about the size of and the distance away of the object to be grasped, etc.)

Head	Body Parts
______________________	______________________
______________________	______________________
______________________	______________________
______________________	______________________
______________________	______________________
______________________	______________________

2. Read 1 Corinthians 12:12–31 and determine the main theme of each part of the passage:

   Verses 12–13 ______________________________________

   Verses 14–20 ______________________________________

   Verses 21–26 ______________________________________

   Verses 27–31 ______________________________________

Note the word "church" in verse 28. What is the significance of it being used here?

____

____

____

3. What persons make up the church (the body of Christ) today?

____

____

What is the difference between the terms: the *visible church* and the *invisible church*?

____

____

4. Apply the specific facts of how your physical head and body relate to each other over to the spiritual relationship between Christ—the Head—and a believer (or with all believers).

____

____

____

5. What specific functions (gifts) are given to various members of the church (Christ's body)?

Ephesians 4:11–13 ______________________________

____

1 Corinthians 12:27–31 ______________________________

____

1 Peter 4:10–11 ______________________________

____

Romans 12:4–8 ______________________________

____

6. From the gifts (or functions) listed in these scriptures, can you identify your own specific gift(s) that enables you to minister or contribute as a member of Christ's body?

____

____

____

7. Within your own local congregation, can you identify the gifts of other individuals? How have they been exercised for the well-being of the whole congregation?

____

____

____

8. Are there some believers who are without any specific gift? (See 1 Corinthians 12:7.)

____

____

9. Here are some additional scriptures pertinent to this analogy:

   Ephesians 1:22–23; 4:15–16, 25 ______________________________

   ____

   Colossians 1:18, 2:19, 3:15 _________________________________

   ____

10. For an additional study, check a concordance for verses referring to "one another" to learn the Bible's teaching about the interdependence and interaction between the members of Christ's body. Make a list of the church's intended functions from those verses.

Reflection

What can we learn from this analogy that will help us to grow in our relationship with Christ?

Read, sing, or listen to one of the following songs:

- "Blest Be the Tie That Binds"
- "We Are God's People"
- "We Are One in the Bond of Love"
- or ____

As an individual member of Christ's body, what would be an appropriate prayer for you to offer to the great Head of the Church?

The Father and the Child

Both a father and a mother provide the best combination for the parenting of a child because each parent makes a distinctive contribution to the raising of a child. The role of the father is to be a courageous protector, a loving provider, and one who sets an example of moral leadership. Legally he is a father; lovingly he is a dad. Although some persons may not have had a positive role model in their own father, this scriptural analogy presents a strong, caring God as the Father of his children.

1. Describe the differences between the roles of a father and a child:

Father	Child
__________	__________
__________	__________
__________	__________
__________	__________
__________	__________
__________	__________

2. What are the only ways that a person becomes the child of a parent?

   How are these both true in becoming a child of God?

   ---

3. Read John 1:12 and John 3:1–7. Compare a spiritual birth with a natural birth.

____

____

4. What more can we discover about being children of God in the following scriptures?

   Romans 8:16–17 ______________________________

   ____

   Galatians 3:29, 4:7 ___________________________

   ____

   "Because they are children (sons), they are also ____________."

5. After reading Matthew 26:39 and Mark 14:35–36, how did Jesus come to terms with his Father's authority?

   ____

   ____

   ____

   ____

   What does that teach us about our attitude toward our heavenly Father's authority?

   ____

   ____

   ____

   ____

6. Christ's parable of the prodigal son in Luke 15:11–32 is a poignant account of a loving father and a wayward son. Identify the main teaching points in the parable about the relationship between a loving God and a penitent sinner.

____

____

____

____

____

____

____

____

7. Examine 1 John 3:1–2 to learn about the ultimate culmination of the relationship between the heavenly Father and his children.

____

____

____

____

____

____

____

Reflection

What can we learn from this analogy of the Father and his child that will help us to grow in our relationship with Christ?

____

____

____

____

____

____

Read, sing, or listen to one of the following songs:

- "Children of the Heavenly Father"
- "The Family of God"
- "My Father and I"
- "Getting Used to the Family"
- "A Child of the King"
- "Plenty of Room in the Family"
- or ____

How might a child of God appropriately pray to such a gracious and glorious Father?

The Potter and the Clay

The basics of pottery making have not changed much over the centuries. A potter sits at a spinning wheel with a lump of wet clay, with some water and a few simple tools nearby. With deft hands, the potter gradually shapes the clay into a vessel that matches the desired image in his mind. In time, he produces a finished piece that reflects his artistry, skill, and patience. The teaching values in this analogy are as applicable today as they were in ancient times.

1. Read the following scriptures and record some observations:

   Isaiah 29:16, 45:9, 64:8; Jeremiah 18:1–6

   In the above passages, who is represented by "the clay"?

   Why do you believe that God chose to refer to them in this way?

   ____

   ____

   What connection may there be between Jeremiah 1:5 and the potter/clay analogy?

   ____

   ____

   ____

2. Read Romans 9:20–21. Is this analogy used differently in this passage from that in the Old Testament? ______________________

   ____

   ____

   Is it a fair interpretation of scripture to apply the potter/clay relationship to today's believers?

   ____

   ____

... and to you? ____

____

3. Have you ever worked clay as a potter or seen a potter at work? If so, what light can those experiences shed upon the truths imbedded in this analogy? ____

____

____

____

Can you add to the following respective significance of both sides in this analogy?

The Potter	**The Clay**
• must have imagination and creativity. • must have a design in mind. • never gives up on the clay and may have to "reknead" it or correct its composition. • exerts pressure on the clay to produce the desired results.	• is under the control of the potter. • is lowly material and has little value in its raw state. • must be responsive to the potter's touch. • must take no credit to itself for what it becomes.
• ______________________	• ______________________
• ______________________	• ______________________
• ______________________	• ______________________

4. There is great value in our being shaped by God into a person of significance and beauty, and into one who fulfills God's purpose in creating us. God is at work fashioning a corporate body of

believers—comprised of individuals who become both functional and beautiful. Read and reflect upon Ephesians 2:10: "We are his workmanship ..."

5. Can the pressure exerted by the potter be compared to the pressure of discipline and suffering experienced by every believer? Discover the value of discipline in Hebrews 12, as well as its painful effect.

6. Share some comments and observations about life changes and character formation brought about by the Master Potter's work in believers' lives.

7. In this potter/clay analogy, how do the twin themes of divine sovereignty and our human will interact?

____

____

____

____

Reflection

Read, sing, or listen to one of the following songs:

- "Have Thine Own Way, Lord"
- "Something Beautiful"
- "He's Still Workin' on Me"
- "The Potter and the Clay"
- "Change My Heart, O God"
- or ____

As you consider yourself as clay in the Potter's hands, what might be an appropriate prayer for you to offer to the Divine Potter?

The Vine and the Branch

The climate and terrain of much of the Bible lands were especially suited for the growing of grapes. The early Israelites found vineyards already growing when they came to inhabit the land of Canaan. There are many references to vineyards throughout both Old and New Testaments. While the juice of the grapes provided a basic beverage, grapes were also an important source of sugar. The entire process of cultivating and harvesting grapes in ancient culture was familiar and well understood.

1. Read John 15:1–11, 16. In this passage, what are the four parts in this analogy?

    ____branch____ ________________

    ____gardener____ ________________

2. How would a botanist or a gardener describe the actual connection between the vine and a branch? ______________________________

____

____

How would that be similar to one's relationship with Christ? _____

____

____

____

3. What aspect of grape cultivation is described in John 15:2, 6? Why is that included in Christ's teaching of this analogy? ____________

____

____

____

4. What is meant by "pruning" in our relationship with Christ? _____

____

____

____

Can you identify or describe such "pruning" in your own life? ____

____

____

____

____

5. What is the fruit that God desires to produce (and is expecting) in each believer's life?

Fruit in a believer's life = ?

Matthew 22:37 ____

Revelation 3:20 ____

Matthew 6:2–4 ____

Mark 16:15 ____

Galatians 5:22–23 ____

Romans 1:13 ____

Hebrews 13:15 ____

Other ____

6. In the passage of John 15:4–7, what verb occurs most frequently?

____

Count the number of times that verb occurs. ________________

Why is that verb relevant in the vine/branch analogy? __________

____

____

(Compare.also: 1 John 2:24, 27–28; 3:6, 24; 4:13–16; 2 John 9.)

7. Have you seen televised accounts of conjoined twins? Does that condition of such a "mutual indwelling" of two persons accurately describe the relationship between Christ and a believer?

   If not, why not? ______________________________

   ____

   If so, what can you imply from it? ______________________________

   ____

   ____

8. Here are other scriptures that are pertinent to the vine/branch relationship; select one or two and compare them to Christ's teaching about the vine and branch:

   Psalm 80:8–13   Romans 6:20–23   Isaiah 5:1–7
   Galatians 5:22–23   Jeremiah 2:20–22   Ephesians 5:9

Reflection

What truths in this analogy will help us grow in our relationship with Christ?

____

____

____

____

____

Sing, read, or listen to one of the following songs:

- "O Jesus Christ, Grow Thou in Me"
- "The Vine"
- "Let the Beauty of Jesus Be Seen in Me"
- or, ____

Knowing that God expects fruit to be produced in you, compose an appropriate prayer to be offered to the Master Gardener: ___________

The Groom and the Bride

After a hubbub of detailed planning and arranging for their wedding, the bride and groom exchange their ceremonial vows with deep emotion. They begin life's most intimate and loving relationship by making a lifelong covenant with each other, which is both exclusive and unconditional, using words such as: "for better or worse," "unto you only," and "from this day forward until death shall part us." Their covenant commitment is blessed by a prayer, and the marriage contract is legally recorded. This momentous occasion now calls for a jubilant celebration with family and friends.

1. In the following Old Testament references, what is God's relationship with the people of Israel?

   Isaiah 54:5–8 ______________________________

   ____

   Jeremiah 3:14, 20 ______________________________

   ____

   Hosea 2:19–20 ______________________________

   ____

2. Examine how these New Testament portions contribute to this same relationship analogy. To whom is Christ likened?

   Matthew 9:14–15 ______________________________

   ____

   John 3:28–29 ______________________________

   ____

   2 Corinthians 11:1–2 ______________________________

   ____

3. Read Ephesians 5:22–33. What is taught here about the deeper spiritual significance of the marriage relationship between a husband and a wife?

   ____

   ____

4. Why do Roman Catholic nuns wear a wedding band? What is your view on this?

5. As married life begins for a couple, what changes or adjustments do they make (or should make) in their living that are different from when they were single?

   How might such changes apply to our relationship with Christ?

6. What does the parable in Matthew 25:1–13 teach us about our betrothed relationship with Christ?

7. Examine Revelation 19:6–9 to discover the future and eternal relevance in our spiritual "engagement" or betrothed relationship with our Lord. (Could these verses suggest why brides' gowns are traditionally white?)

8. What factors that make for a strong, loving marriage could also be applied to strengthening and deepening our own personal relationship with the Lord?

Reflection

What can we learn from this analogy that will help us grow in our relationship with Christ?

Read, sing, or listen to one of the following songs:

- "Jesus, Lover of My Soul"
- "My Jesus, I Love Thee"
- "In Love with the Lover of My Soul"
- "O Perfect Love"
- "Jesus, the Very Thought of Thee"
- "I Love You, Lord"
- or ______________________________

Remembering your sacred vow of commitment and consecration to Christ, and the love that binds you together, what prayer would you offer to the Divine Bridegroom?

The Master and the Servant

Slavery in the United States has been officially abolished for over 150 years, having been practiced elsewhere in the world for centuries. Dominating control by one person or group over another has marked civilization's history—even to our present time—whether by governments or groups, or by individuals who wield controlling power. Although we now live in a more enlightened age, every person experiences some form of servitude, even as an employee or in military service. Sometimes a person will offer to volunteer to become a servant, giving freely of his or her time, energy, and resources for some cause. And an individual may even commit to serve for a lifetime in some ministry.

1. From your understanding of servitude in history (slavery or otherwise), describe the relationship between a master and his servant.

Master	Servant
________________	________________
________________	________________
________________	________________
________________	________________
________________	________________
________________	________________

2. Note the parables of Jesus that use the master/servant relationship as a basis in their narrative:

   Matthew 20:1–16—parable of the vineyard workers
   Matthew 21:33–41—parable of the wicked tenants
   Luke 12:42–48—parable of the unwise stewards

   To whom do these parables refer to as the landowner? __________

3. Read John 13:1–17. In this passage, what kind of relationship did Christ expect between himself and his disciples?

   ____

   ____

   ____

What task did Jesus perform, and why?

____

____

____

4. After reading Philippians 2:5–8, what connection may there be between that passage and the John 13:1–17 passage?

____

____

____

____

5. How does Paul refer to himself in the following verses, and why?

Romans 1:1 ________________________________

Philippians 1:1 ____________________________

Titus 1:1 _________________________________

Philemon verse 1 ___________________________

6. What is the meaning of the title "Lord," when referring to Jesus Christ, and what do these scriptures teach about its use?

Matthew 7:21–23 ___________________________

____

____

Luke 6:46 ______________________________

____

____

7. Read Romans 6:15–23. Consider what this passage teaches about spiritual servitude and about its bondage and the means of emancipation.

The former life		The new life
slaves to ________		slaves to ________
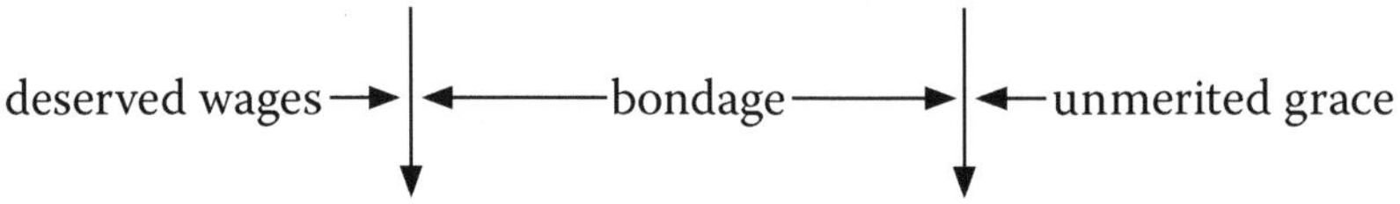 deserved wages →	← bondage →	← unmerited grace
immediate effect?		immediate effect?
________		________
ultimate result?		ultimate result?
________		________

8. When is the only time that a slave's master could not have control over his servant? Reflect upon this truth in Romans 6:5–14.

____

What does this truth mean in your own relationship with Christ?

____

____

Reflection

Prayerfully read Romans 12:1–2.

Sing, read, or listen to one of the following songs:

- "He Is Lord"
- "I Call Him Lord"
- "Jesus Is Lord of All"
- "Then I Met the Master"
- "Give of Your Best to the Master"
- "Master Speak, Thy Servant Heareth"
- "Ye Servants of God, Your Master Proclaim"
- or ______________________
- "My Wonderful Lord"
- "The Longer I Serve Him"
- "More Like the Master"
- "Make Me A Captive, Lord"
- "What Shall I Give Thee, Master?"
- "O Master Let Me Walk with Thee"

9. Knowing the absolute authority of the Lord of Lords, what would be an appropriate prayer for one of his servants to offer?

The Cornerstone and the Building Stone

Although the cornerstone in a building today may be just an embellishment, in ancient times a cornerstone marked the starting location of a building—where construction would begin. All building stones were then laid plumb with that cornerstone, so the building would be properly constructed. Because the use of stone in buildings was common in Jesus's time, this analogy was readily understood.

1. Before any excavation is done, how is a new building's location today marked on a specific site?

____

____

____

____

____

____

2. Read Isaiah 28:14–17 and Psalm 118:21–24. What promise does God give to Israel, and why?

____

____

____

____

____

3. How does Jesus interpret that promise from Psalm 118 in Matthew 21:42–46? (Similarly, in Mark 12:10–11 and Luke 20:17–18.)

____

____

4. What is Peter's interpretation of the promise in Psalm 118 and in Acts 4:8–12?

5. Read 1 Peter 2:4–10. How does Peter expand the analogy to Christ as the cornerstone? What other stones are mentioned?

6. In 1 Peter 2:8, what other type of stone is Christ called? Why?

7. Read Ephesians 2:19–22. With Christ being the chief cornerstone, what building is being constructed? (Compare 1 Corinthians 3:11–17, 6:19; 2 Corinthians 6:16.)

8. Consider and discuss how this cornerstone/building stone analogy can be applied to our own relationship with Christ. How are individual believers "built" into a temple? In actual construction, stones are passively placed into a building by a builder. Do "living stones" have an active role in their placement? If so, how?

9. How can you reconcile 1 Corinthians 3:16 and Ephesians 2:21–22 with Revelation 21:22?

Reflection

What can we learn from this analogy that will help us grow in our relationship with Christ?

Sing, read, or listen to one of the following songs:

- "The Cornerstone"
- "Christ Is Made the Sure Foundation"
- "Built on the Rock"
- "We Are God's People"
- "My Hope Is Built"
- or ____

In realizing that you are a living component in God's ultimate mission in this world, and that he has chosen to include you in this noble task, what would be an appropriate prayer for you to offer to your Cornerstone?

The Friend and the Friend

We value our friends more than any material possession. Along with our family, the special bonds with our friends lie closest to our hearts. What brings two persons together to form a bond of friendship? How do two persons just happen to "hit it off" with each other and not as much with another person?

1. Can you add to the following characteristics of friendship?

    - pleasure in each other's company
    - a caring concern for each other's best interests

- confidentiality
- loyal support and sympathy
- sharing common interests, causes, or struggles

____

____

2. Read the following verses to note the special designation given to Abraham.

   2 Chronicles 20:7 Isaiah 41:8 James 2:23

   Abraham is called ______________________________

3. Why was Abraham referred to that way?

   Examine these scriptures to discover reasons for his favor with God:

   Genesis 11:31, 12:9, 15:1–5, 18 Hebrews 11:8–10, 17–19

   ____

   ____

   ____

   ____

4. Was anyone else in the Bible referred to in the same way? See Exodus 33:11.

   ____

   ____

5. Describe the friendship between David and Jonathan as described in the following passages: 1 Samuel 18:1–4, 19:1–7, 20:1–42.

____

____

____

6. Read John 15:11–17. What is the situation in which these verses are found?

____

____

To whom is Jesus speaking, and when and where?

____

____

____

Notice in John 15:15 how Jesus somewhat redefines his relationship with his disciples.

____

____

____

7. Read John 15:13. To what extent may friendship go?

____

____

Can you foresee that your relationship with a friend might go that far?

In a military context, when is John 15:13 most often quoted? Is the application of that verse in that way appropriate? Why?

Reflection

Read, sing, or listen to one of these songs:

- "Jesus Is All the World to Me"
- "What a Friend We Have in Jesus"
- "Friendship with Jesus"
- "He's a Friend of Mine"
- "Our Great Savior"
- "No, Not One"
- "I've Found a Friend"
- "Saved, Saved"

- "I Remember Calvary"
- "The Lily of the Valley"
- or ____

Because there are close ties of friendship between you and Jesus, what would be an appropriate prayer to offer him?

____

____

____

____

____

____

____

____

____

____

Summary

Going back to the first study in Matthew 11:28–30

1. In "coming" and "taking" Christ's yoke, can you identify that turning point of conversion in your life and what may have led up to it?

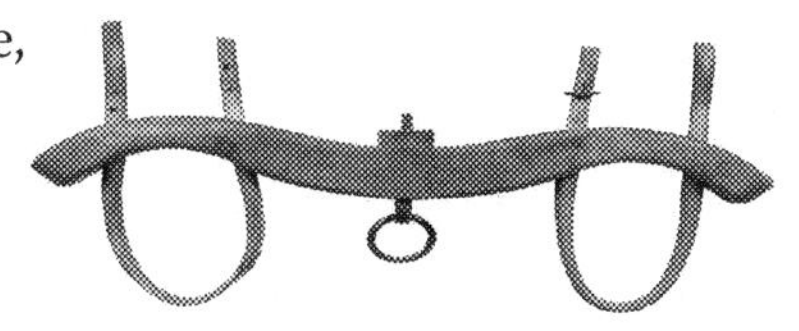

2. In "learning" of Christ—about his person and about his teachings—what most helps you in your learning?

   - personal Bible study and devotions?
   - teachings, sermons at your church?
   - radio, TV programs, books, or recorded teachings?
   - being in some special group or fellowship?
   - or ______________________________
   - or ______________________________

3. The word *disciple* means to be "a learner, a student, or one being taught." What name do you use of yourself to others to identify your relationship with Christ?

   I'm ... "a disciple,"
   "a servant of the Lord,"
   "a Christian,"
   "a convert,"
   "an evangelical,"
   "a child of God,"
   "a believer,"
   "a follower of Christ,"
   "______________________________"
   or "______________________________"

4. How would you define the "rest" promised by Christ? Can you suggest other meanings than the following ones:

   - the refreshment of one's soul.
   - release from the burden of guilt and condemnation.
   - a deep confidence in God's overshadowing care.
   - an inner renewal of strength.
   - rest over a victory achieved.
   - an awareness of being in alignment with God's will.

   ____

   ____

   Would there be any connection between Jeremiah 6:16 and Christ's promise of rest?

   ____

   ____

   ____

Of all the relationship analogies studied, which one, or ones, had the most personal relevance to you?

___

___

___

___

___

Points to Ponder

- As a yokefellow with Jesus, does his sharing of my cares of life make them less difficult?

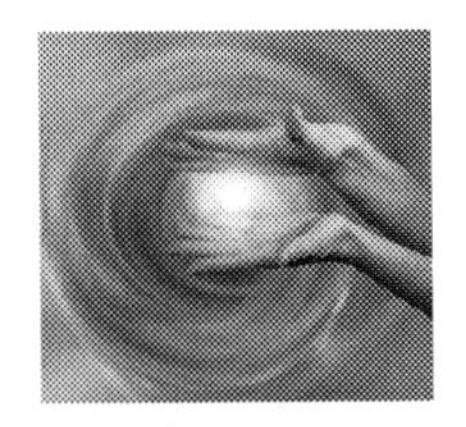

- As a specially created person, am I reflecting the great glory of the Creator?

- As a dependent sheep in Christ's fold, do I follow my Shepherd's leadership?

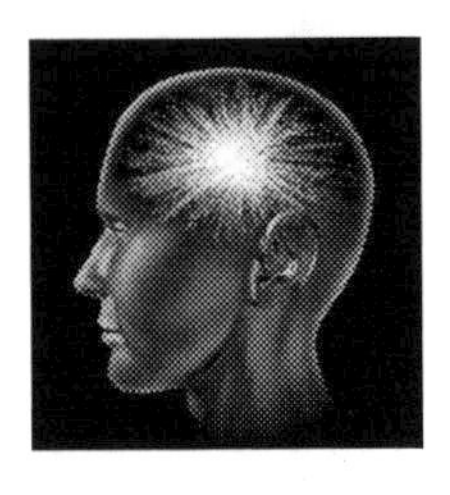

- As an integral working member of Christ's body, am I responding to the divine impulses of the Head?

- As a child of a mighty and loving Father, am I obedient to his directives for my life?

- As a lump of formable humanity, am I pliable in the deft hands of the Potter?

- As a growing extension of the living Vine, how am I being productive as he intends?

- As a betrothed fiancée to my Lord, am I living in faithfulness to that commitment?

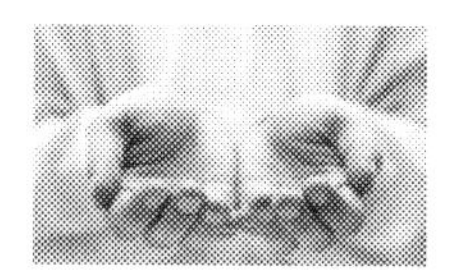

- As a willing servant of my Master, am I being obedient to his instructions and commands?

- As an individual component in the structure of the church, am I willing to be placed and used anywhere the Builder may choose?

- As a personal friend of Christ, am I loyal to and supportive of him?

Reflection

William Cowper (1731–1800), an English poet of the evangelical revival, penned the words of this prayer-hymn. Perhaps we can make it ours:

O for a closer walk with God,
A calm and heav'nly frame,
A light to shine upon the road
That leads me to the Lamb.

Where is the blessedness I knew
When first I saw the Lord?
Where is the soul-refreshing view
Of Jesus, and his word?

What peaceful hours I once enjoy'd!
How sweet their mem'ry still!
But they have left an aching void,
The world can never fill.

Return, O holy Dove, return,
Sweet messenger of rest,
I hate the sins that made thee mourn,
And drove thee from my breast.

The dearest idol I have known,
Whate'er that idol be,
Help me to tear it from thy throne,
And worship only thee.

So shall my walk be close with God,
Calm and serene my frame,
So purer light shall mark the road
That leads me to the Lamb.

While some may believe that to gain a closer walk with God may mean to become a member of some church, consent to some statement of faith, engage in some demanding discipline, or support some worthy cause, it is in reality, meeting and knowing God personally, and living in a relationship with him from day to day.

About the Author

James A. Blaine is an ordained minister in the Wesleyan Church, and has served as pastor for 40+ years in Wesleyan and United Methodist churches in the United States and Canada. He has also had teaching experiences in church conferences and local churches.

He is a graduate of Marion College (now, Indiana Wesleyan University), and of Asbury Theological Seminary (KY). He has earned the M.Th. post-graduate seminary degree at Western Theological Seminary (MI), majoring in biblical literature.

He and his wife, Wandalou, were caregivers for 58 years for their older son (now deceased) who was injured at birth with cerebral palsy. They have a grown son and daughter who live in New York.

Acknowledgements

I am indebted to my college and seminary professors who inspired me to have a love for God's Word, the Bible.

For using his computer expertise to coach and assist me, and for his kind support throughout, I am much indebted to Dr. Robert G. Willhoft. He is my son-in-law, and Professor of Computer Science at Roberts Wesleyan College, North Chili, New York.

Printed in the United States
By Bookmasters